T0327894

BERLIN

BERLIN

Photos by Thomas Kierok

BRAUN

Berlin ist schnell, schillernd und ständig in Bewegung – und damit eine permanente Herausforderung für seine Bewohner und Besucher. Wer sich ein Bild von dieser rasanten Stadt machen möchte, begibt sich auf eine abenteuerliche Reise. Um Berlin wirklich kennenzulernen, muss man in die Metropole eintauchen und sich auf die nahezu unendliche Vielfalt an Impressionen einlassen, mit denen sie Neugierige in ihren Bann zieht.

Kaum eine andere Stadt hat in den letzten 20 Jahren derart schnelle und umfassende Veränderung erfahren wie Berlin. Neues traf dabei stets auf gewachsene Strukturen. So entstand und entsteht fortwährend eine atemberaubende Mixtur aus Historie und Hipness, Beschleunigung und Verfall, oft Tür an Tür. Veränderung geschieht mal zur Freude, mal zum Erstaunen, mal ist sie Kunst, mal Provokation – aber etwas ist sie immer: ein Stück Berlin, lebendig, unaufhaltsam und mit allen Sinnen erlebbar. Die vielen Gesichter dieser einzigartigen Metropole lassen niemanden kalt. Wie aber kann man sich ihrer Präsenz angemessen nähern? Wie den Puls der Stadt fühlen und ihre schillernden Facetten einfangen?

Eben dieser Herausforderung hat sich der Berliner Fotograf Thomas Kierok mit seiner Kamera gestellt. Und zwar auf ganz eigene Weise. Kieroks Fotografien halten die Gegensätze fest, die Berlin definieren. Neu ist die Art der Komposition: Dazu werden je zwei Abbildungen auf einer Doppelseite gegenüber gestellt. Dabei bezeugen die Motivpaare nicht bloß einen simplen Kontrast, sondern bilden das Muster komplementärer Erfahrungen ab – Erfahrungen in ein und derselben Stadt. Berlin bleibt Berlin. Darum gibt es, so unterschiedlich die Motive auch sein mögen, immer etwas, das sie miteinander verbindet.

Jedes Bild und jede Szene steht für sich, und verweist doch über sich hinaus. Ein ganz eigener Sog entsteht: Während jedes Motiv das Auge zum Verweilen einlädt, zieht es den Betrachter zugleich weiter zum nächsten Bild. Dadurch wird Berlin nicht als Summe isolierter Momentaufnahmen dokumentiert, sondern erscheint als Schmelztiegel, als unentwirrbares Konglomerat von Architektur, Szenen, Menschen und Stimmungen über die verschiedenen Jahres- und Tageszeiten hinweg. Ein pulsierendes und atmendes Gesamtkunstwerk voller Widersprüche und Parallelen entsteht. Berlin, das ist große Geschichte und der kleine Mann unterm Fernsehturm. Berlin ist Bundestag und Boulette, Unter den Linden und die U-Bahn, es ist Weltpolitik und Würstchenbude. Wenn Berühmtes neben Unbekanntem erscheint, verwandelt das Prinzip der ergänzenden Gegenüberstellung auch den Blick auf die scheinbar längst bekannten Bauten, Plätze und Straßenszenen. Postkartenmotive werden neu erfahrbar – wie in einem Kaleidoskop, bei dem eine leichte Drehung genügt, um die immer gleichen Elemente nie gesehene Figuren hervorbringen zu lassen.

Berlin ist eines der prominentesten politischen und kulturellen Zentren Europas, ein temporeicher Brennpunkt der Hypermoderne. Gleichzeitig bekennt sich die Stadt aber auch mit Souveränität und einem Augenzwinkern zu Oasen der Beschaulichkeit und Orten von eigentümlichem und eigensinnigem Widerstand. Ob piefig oder punk, Berlin bleibt herzlich. Der Betrachter ist eingeladen, sich auf all das einzulassen. Bei einem spannenden und überraschenden Gang durch die Stadt wird er Neues entdecken, Altes wiedererkennen und in jedem Fall Vieles ganz anders sehen.

Markus Sebastian Braun

Berlin is fast, dazzling, and constantly in motion – a perpetual challenge for its inhabitants and its visitors. Anyone who tries to get a clear picture of the city is truly in for a ride. The only way to really get to know Berlin is to dive into the metropolis and let yourself be taken over by the infinite variety of captivating impressions.

Hardly any other city has experienced such rapid and all-encompassing changes as Berlin has in the last twenty years. Everywhere in the city, new is met with old, creating a breath-taking mix of the historical and the hip, acceleration and decline, sometimes right next door to each other. Change is sometimes joyous, sometimes shocking, and it can be art or provocation – but one sure thing is that it is always a part of Berlin: lively, irresistible and an experience for all the senses. The many sides of this exceptional metropolis won't leave anyone cold. But how best to approach it? How can one feel the very pulse of this city, and capture its dazzling facets?

This is the very challenge that Thomas Kierok, a photographer from Berlin, has taken on. In their own way, his photographs succeed in capturing the contradictions that define Berlin. The composition is innovative: two photographs are laid out on each double page. Each pair of images presents more than a simple contrast, creating a pattern of complementary experiences – both possible in the very same city. Berlin being Berlin, no matter how different the images seem on the surface, there is always a connection.

Each picture and each scene stands alone, but also has meaning beyond that single image. The effect is compelling. Every photo invites the eye to linger but simultaneously draws the viewer on to the next image. This means Berlin is not documented as the sum of individual snapshots, but as a melting pot that inextricably mixes architecture, scenes, people and moods over different seasons and times of day. A vibrant, breathing work of art filled with contradictions and parallels results, Berlin is its great history as well as the everyday citizen in the shadow of the TV tower. Berlin is Bundestag and Boulette, Unter den Linden and the subway, it is world politics and snack stands. If the unknown appears next to the famous, the principle of complementary opposition also transforms the view of the renowned buildings, plazas and streets. Postcard scenes can be experienced in a new way- as a kaleidoscope, where the slightest turn is enough bring out new features in the unchanging elements.

Berlin is one of the most prominent political and cultural centers of Europe, a fast-paced nexus of hyper-modernity. At the same time, the stately city is still home to winking oases of tranquility as well as peculiar places of stubborn resistance. Whether bourgeois or punk, Berlin is always sincere, and observers are invited to get involved. In this exciting and surprising journey through the city, you will discover what's new, recognize the old, and inevitably see it all in a whole new light.

Markus Sebastian Braun

008 . An den Treptowers, Treptow

Holzmarktstraße, Friedrichshain . 411

412 . Columbiadamm, Tempelhof

414 . View towards Potsdamer Platz, Mitte

Kastanienallee, Prenzlauer Berg . 415

The Deutsche Nationalbibliothek lists this publication in the Deutsche Nationalbibliografie; detailed bibliographical data are available on the internet at http://dnb.d-nb.de.

ISBN 978-3-03768-090-2

© 2012 by Braun Publishing AG
www.braun-publishing.ch

1st edition 2012

Editor: Markus Sebastian Braun
Photos: Thomas Kierok, Berlin
Editorial staff: Nicole Felhösi, Anne Osherson, Manuela Roth
Graphic concept and layout: Manuela Roth, Berlin
Reproduction: Bild1Druck, Berlin
Photos Cover, Backcover: Thomas Kierok, Berlin
Photos on page 25, 29, 30, 37, 53, 58, 130, 131, 132, 134, 135, 144, 145, 146 147, 148, 149, 150, 151, 152, 153, 156, 157, 158, 159, 160, 161, 164, 165, 166, 167, 169, 174, 176, 178, 179, 182, 184, 185, 187, 188, 189, 190, 191, 194, 196, 197, 198, 199, 200, 201, 202, 204, 208, 209, 210, 211, 212, 259, 265, 267, 276, 284, 312, 325, 348, 349, 353, 356, 370, 371, 378, 379, 380, 381, 382, 383 stem from the archive of the publishing house.

Tunnelstraße, Friedrichshain . 009

HIER WOHNTE
GEORG
SALINGER
JG. 1892
DEPORTIERT 1943
AUSCHWITZ
ERMORDET

HIER WOHNTE
ROSA
SALINGER
GEB. GINSBERG
JG. 1893
DEPORTIERT 1943
AUSCHWITZ
ERMORDET

HIER WOHNTE
URSULA
SALINGER
GEB. SALINGER
JG. 1919
DEPORTIERT 1942
RIGA
ERMORDET

HIER WOHNTE
GERD
SALINGER
JG. 1922
DEPORTIERT 1943
AUSCHWITZ
ERMORDET

010 . Rosenthaler Straße, Mitte

Neue Synagoge, Oranienburger Straße, Mitte . 011

012 . *Berlin Cathedral*, Am Lustgarten, Mitte

Am Lustgarten, Mitte . 013

014 . Gendarmenmarkt, Mitte

Tacheles, Oranienburger Straße, Mitte . 015

016 . Wilhelmstraße, Mitte

Memhardstraße, Mitte . 017

018 . *Memorial to the Murdered Members of the Reichstag*, Platz der Republik, Mitte

Memorial to the Murdered Jews of Europe, Ebertstraße, Mitte . 019

020 . Hackescher Markt, Mitte

Tegel Airport, Reinickendorf . 021

022 . *Berlin Zoo*, Charlottenburg

Stubbenkammerstraße, Prenzlauer Berg . 023

024 . View of *Berlin Cathedral* and *Rotes Rathaus*, Mitte

View towards *Reichstag*, Mitte . 025

026 . Holzmarktstraße, Friedrichshain

Kurfürstendamm, Charlottenburg . 027

028 . Grunerstraße, Mitte

Dorotheenstraße, Mitte . 029

030 . Bergmannstraße, Kreuzberg

Friedrichstraße, Mitte . 031

032 . View towards Potsdamer Platz, Mitte

Potsdamer Platz, Mitte . 033

034 . *Swiss Embassy*, Otto-von-Bismarck-Allee, Mitte

Haus des Lehrers, Alexanderstraße, Mitte . 035

036 . Alexanderstraße, Mitte

ELLEN VON UNWERTH
The Big Show

038 . *Soviet War Memorial*, Treptower Park, Treptow

Soviet War Memorial, Tiergarten . 039

040 . *Reichstag*, Platz der Republik, Mitte

042 . View from Oberbaum Bridge towards Alexanderplatz, Kreuzberg

View from Warschauer Straße towards Alexanderplatz, Friedrichshain . 043

Strausberg Nord
S5 Ahrensfelde
S75 Wartenberg
S3 Erkner

Westkreuz S3
Potsdam Hbf S7
Berlin-Spandau S75
Berlin-Spandau S3

044 . S-Bahn station Hackescher Markt, Mitte

Kastanienallee, Prenzlauer Berg . 045

046 . *Heilandskirche Sacrow*, Fährstraße, Potsdam

View from Reichstagufer towards Schiffbauerdamm, Mitte . 047

048 . Hauptstraße, Rummelsburg

Alexanderplatz, Mitte . 049

050 . Friedrichstraße, Mitte

Reichstagufer, Mitte . 051

052 . Holzmarktstraße, Friedrichshain

Olympic Stadium, Charlottenburg . 053

054 . Alexanderplatz, Mitte

Alexanderplatz, Mitte . 055

056 . Görlitzer Ufer, Kreuzberg

Strausberger Platz, Friedrichshain . 057

058 . *Chapel of Reconciliation*, Bernauer Straße, Mitte

Course of the Wall, Ebertstraße, Mitte . 059

060 . U-Bahn station Schlesisches Tor, Kreuzberg

U-Bahn station Pariser Platz, Mitte . 061

062 . *Humboldt-Box*, Schlossplatz, Mitte

Berlin Cathedral, Am Lustgarten, Mitte . 063

064 . *Bugatti Showroom*, Friedrichstraße, Mitte

Wilhelmstraße / Zimmerstraße, Mitte . 065

066 . Schönhauser Allee / Kastanienallee, Prenzlauer Berg

Wannsee, Zehlendorf . 067

068 . Reichpietschufer, Tiergarten

Leipziger Straße, Mitte . 069

Kurfürstendamm

11-17

070 . Kurfürstendamm, Charlottenburg

072 . *Europa Center*, Breitscheidplatz, Charlottenburg

Alexanderplatz, Mitte . 073

074 . *Embassy of the Russian Federation*, Unter den Linden, Mitte

British Embassy, Wilhelmstraße, Mitte . 075

076 . Holzmarktstraße, Friedrichshain

Holzmarktstraße, Friedrichshain . 077

078 . Kurfürstendamm, Charlottenburg

Strandbad Weißensee, Weißensee . 079

080 . Tiergarten, Tiergarten

YAAM, Mühlenstraße, Friedrichshain . 081

082 . View towards Oberbaum Bridge, Kreuzberg

Boulevard of Stars, Potsdamer Straße, Mitte . 083

084 . Müllerstraße, Wedding

Radio Tower at *ICC*, Charlottenburg . 085

086 . Paul-Lincke-Ufer, Kreuzberg

Sophienstraße, Mitte . 087

088 . *Berlin Wall Memorial*, Bernauer Straße, Mitte

090 . Jewish cemetery, Schönhauser Allee, Prenzlauer Berg

der Tod muß abgeschafft
werden, diese verdammte
Schweinerei muß aufhören.
Wer ein Wort des Trostes
spricht, ist ein Verräter

Bazon Brock

092 . View towards *Club der Visionäre* and *Freischwimmer*, Kreuzberg

Holzmarktstraße, Friedrichshain . 093

094 . Maybachufer, Neukölln

Berliner Philharmonie, Herbert-von-Karajan-Straße, Tiergarten . 095

096 . Gendarmenmarkt, Mitte

Kaiser-Wilhelm-Memorial-Church, Breitscheidplatz, Charlottenburg . 097

098 . Lychener Straße, Prenzlauer Berg

Wilhelmstraße / Zimmerstraße, Mitte . 099

100 . *Brandenburg Gate*, Pariser Platz, Mitte

102 . Alexanderplatz, Mitte

104 . *Radio Tower* at *ICC*, Masurenallee Charlottenburg

Schlesisches Tor, Kreuzberg . 105

106 . Dunckerstraße, Prenzlauer Berg

108 . *Strandbad Wannsee*, Zehlendorf

Dircksenstraße, Mitte . 109

110 . Kurstraße, Mitte

Landsberger Allee, Lichtenberg . 111

112 . *Old National Gallery*, Bodestraße, Mitte

114 . View towards Potsdamer Platz, Mitte

View from Warschauer Straße towards Alexanderplatz, Friedrichshain . 115

116 . *Messe Berlin*, Messedamm, Charlottenburg

Flea market, Boxhagener Platz, Friedrichshain . 117

118 . Rosa Luxemburg-Straße, Mitte

View towards *Berlin Cathedral*, Mitte . 119

120 . *Berlin Cathedral*, Mitte

Berlin Cathedral, Am Lustgarten, Mitte . 121

122 . Alexanderplatz, Mitte

Oranienstraße, Kreuzberg . 123

Was Du
heute kannst
entsorgen ...

124 . Hackescher Markt, Mitte

126 . Christmas Market, Potsdamer Platz, Mitte

Christmas Market, Potsdamer Platz, Mitte . 127

128 . *Berlin Fashionweek*, Bebelplatz, Mitte

Berlin Fashionweek, Bebelplatz, Mitte . 129

130 . Knesebeckstraße, Charlottenburg

Knesebeckstraße, Charlottenburg . 131

132 . Kurfürstendamm, Charlottenburg

Tacheles, Oranienburger Straße, Mitte . 133

134 . Pfaueninsel, Wannsee, Zehlendorf

Schlachtensee, Zehlendorf . 135

138 . *Kaiser-Wilhelm-Memorial-Church*, Breitscheidplatz, Charlottenburg

Old National Gallery, Bodestraße, Mitte . 139

140 . Kurfürstendamm, Charlottenburg

142 . Schlesisches Tor, Kreuzberg

View towards Oberbaum Bridge, Kreuzberg . 143

144 . *Berlin Zoo*, Charlottenburg

Chamäleon Theater, Rosenthaler Straße, Mitte . 145

146 . Oberhaardter Weg, Grunewald

Kurfürstendamm, Charlottenburg . 147

148 . Schönhauser Allee / Danziger Straße, Prenzlauer Berg

Neptune Fountain, Spandauer Straße, Mitte . 149

150 . Open-air cinema, *Volkspark Friedrichshain*, Friedrichshain

Clärchens Ballhaus, Auguststraße, Mitte . 151

152 . *Olympic Stadium*, Olympischer Platz, Charlottenburg

Tucholskystraße, Mitte . 153

154 . Breitscheidplatz, Charlottenburg

Olympic Stadium, Charlottenburg . 155

156 . *Siegessäule*, Großer Stern, Tiergarten

Neptune Fountain, Spandauer Straße, Mitte . 157

158 . Cuvrystraße, Kreuzberg

Bellevue Palace, Spreeweg, Tiergarten . 159

160 . *Berliner Philharmonie*, Herbert-von-Karajan-Straße, Tiergarten

Hackesche Höfe, Rosenthaler Straße, Mitte . 161

162 . Friedrichstraße, Mitte

Berlin Fashionweek, Bebelplatz, Mitte . 163

164 . *Kulturbrauerei*, Schönhauser Allee, Prenzlauer Berg

Charlottenburg Palace, Spandauer Damm, Charlottenburg . 165

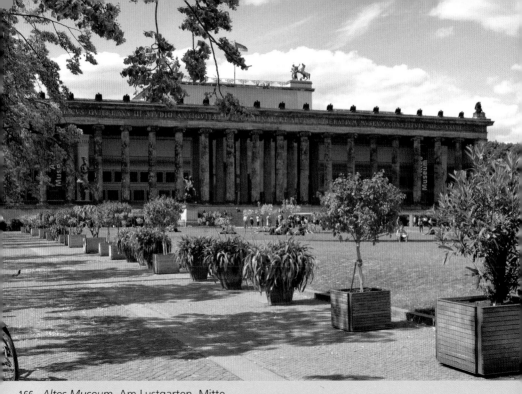

166 . *Altes Museum*, Am Lustgarten, Mitte

Neues Museum, Bodestraße, Mitte . 167

168 . Friedrichstraße, Mitte

S-Bahn station Savignyplatz, Charlottenburg . 169

170 . Alexanderplatz, Mitte

172 . Karl-Lade-Straße, Lichtenberg

Gardens of the World, Eisenacher Straße, Marzahn . 173

174 . *Molecule Man*, An den Treptowers, Treptow

View towards *Narva tower*, Friedrichshain . 175

176 . *Spandau Citadel*, Am Juliusturm, Spandau

Spandau Citadel, Am Juliusturm, Spandau . 177

178 . Memhardstraße, Mitte

Marx-Engels-Forum, Spandauer Straße, Mitte . 179

Am Lustgarten, Mitte . 181

182 . Tucholskystraße, Mitte

184 . *Old National Gallery*, Bodestraße, Mitte

New National Gallery, Potsdamer Straße, Kreuzberg . 185

186 . Oranienstraße, Kreuzberg

Französische Straße, Mitte . 187

188 . Oranienburger Straße, Mitte

Fischerhütte, Schlachtensee, Zehlendorf . 189

190 . Schlachtensee, Zehlendorf

Kantstraße, Charlottenburg . 191

192 . Schlesisches Tor, Kreuzberg

194 . Gendarmenmarkt, Mitte

Volkspark Friedrichshain, Danziger Straße, Friedrichshain . 195

196 . Schlesische Straße, Kreuzberg

Schlesische Straße, Kreuzberg . 197

198 . Oranienburger Straße, Mitte

Deutsche Oper Berlin, Bismarckstraße, Charlottenburg . 199

200 . *TV Tower*, Alexanderplatz, Mitte

Radio Tower at *ICC*, Charlottenburg . 201

202 . Kurfürstendamm, Charlottenburg

Bergmannstraße, Kreuzberg . 203

204 . Kurfürstendamm, Charlottenburg

Stubbenkammerstraße, Prenzlauer Berg . 205

206 . *Carnival of Cultures*, Kreuzberg

Carnival of Cultures, Kreuzberg . 207

208 . View towards *Reichstag*, Mitte

Auguststraße, Mitte . 209

210 . View towards *Nikolaiviertel*, Mitte

Palasstraße, Schöneberg . 211

212 . Captive Balloon *HiFlyer*, Wilhelmstraße / Zimmerstraße, Mitte

214 . *Checkpoint Charlie*, Friedrichstraße, Mitte

Ebertstraße, Mitte . 215

216 . Holzmarktstraße, Friedrichshain

100 S+U-Bahnhof
Zoolog. Garten

be Berlin

Scheidemanstraße, Tiergarten . 217

218 . *Hotel de Rome*, Behrenstraße, Mitte

Alte Schönhauser Straße, Mitte . 219

220 . Karl-Marx-Straße, Neukölln

222 . Maybachufer, Neukölln

224 . Kastanienallee, Prenzlauer Berg

Strandbad Weißensee, Weißensee . 225

226 . *Sony Center*, Potsdamer Platz, Mitte

Berlin Central Station, Mitte . 227

228 . Mühlenstraße, Friedrichshain

Strandbad Weißensee, Weißensee . 229

230 . *Monbijou Park*, Mitte

Holzmarktstraße, Friedrichshain . 231

232 . Alexanderplatz, Mitte

Altes Museum, Am Lustgarten, Mitte . 233

234 . *Tempelhofer Park*, Tempelhof

Tempelhofer Park, Tempelhof . 235

236 . Alexanderplatz, Mitte

Schluss mit Krimi.
Cannabis normal.
www.hanfverband.de

238 . Kastanienallee, Prenzlauer Berg

240 . *Berlin Wall Memorial*, Bernauer Straße, Mitte

Course of the Wall, Ebertstraße, Mitte . 241

Ampelmännchen . 243

244 . *Zeughaus*, Unter den Linden, Mitte

Checkpoint Charlie, Friedrichstraße, Mitte . 245

246 . Tucholskystraße, Mitte

Tacheles, Oranienburger Straße, Mitte . 247

248 . Karl-Marx Allee, Friedrichshain

250 . Hackescher Markt, Mitte

Kaiser-Wilhelm-Memorial-Church, Breitscheidplatz, Charlottenburg . 251

252 . Unter den Linden, Mitte

galerie koal

MARTIN FLEMMING

254 . Bebelplatz, Mitte

Hackesche Höfe, Rosenthaler Straße, Mitte . 255

256 . *Reichstag*, Platz der Republik, Mitte

Dome of the Reichstag, Platz der Republik, Mitte . 257

258 . Alexanderplatz, Mitte

Glienicke Bridge, Wannsee, Zehlendorf . 259

260 . Alexanderplatz, Mitte

Memhardstraße, Mitte . 261

262 . Münzstraße, Mitte

264 . View towards *Molecule Man*, Oberbaum Bridge and Alexanderplatz

Babelsberg Palace, Im Park Babelsberg, Potsdam-Babelsberg . 265

266 . Friedrichstraße, Mitte

Kino in der
KULTURBRAUEREI

268 . *Kulturbrauerei*, Schönhauser Allee, Prenzlauer Berg

270 . *Berlinale Palast*, Potsdamer Platz, Mitte

Berlinale Palast, Potsdamer Platz, Mitte . 271

272 . *Boulevard of Stars*, Potsdamer Straße, Mitte

Berlinale Palast, Potsdamer Platz, Mitte . 273

274 . *Berlinale Palast*, Potsdamer Platz, Mitte

276 . Potsdamer Platz, Mitte

278 . Christmas Market, Spandauer Straße, Mitte

Alexanderplatz, Mitte . 279

280 . Raumerstraße, Prenzlauer Berg

Kastanienallee, Prenzlauer Berg . 281

282 . Raumerstraße, Prenzlauer Berg

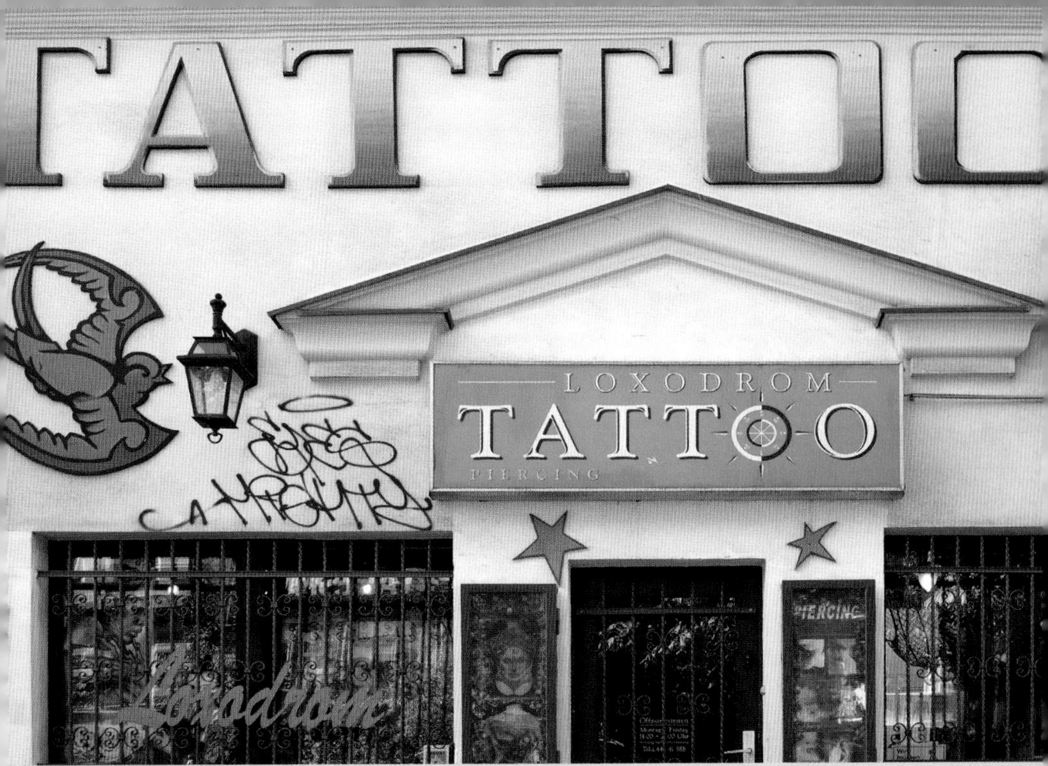

Kastanienallee, Prenzlauer Berg .

284 . *Federal Chancellery*, Willy-Brandt-Straße, Tiergarten

Skalitzer Straße, Kreuzberg . 285

286 . Adalbertstraße, Kreuzberg

288 . Kottbusser Damm, Kreuzberg

Spandauer Straße, Mitte . 289

290 . *Badeschiff*, Eichenstraße, Treptow

Grand Hyatt Berlin, Marlene-Dietrich-Platz, Tiergarten . 291

292 . Senefelder Straße, Prenzlauer Berg

Strandbad Weißensee, Weißensee . 293

294 . Potsdamer Platz, Mitte

Kochstraße / Friedrichstraße, Kreuzberg . 295

296 . Tiergarten, Tiergarten

Christopher Street-Day . 299

schwul

lesbisch

transsexuel

300 . *Christopher Street-Day*, Pariser Platz, Mitte

304 . *Berlin Zoo*, Charlottenburg

306 . Alexanderplatz, Mitte

308 . Pariser Platz, Mitte

310 . Potsdamer Platz, Mitte

Niederbarnimstraße, Friedrichshain . 311

312 . Potsdamer Straße, Tiergarten

Tauentzienstraße, Charlottenburg . 313

314 . Karl-Marx Allee, Mitte

Charlottenburg Palace, Spandauer Damm, Charlottenburg . 315

316 . *Monbijou Park*, Stadtbahnbogen, Mitte

East Side Gallery, Mühlenstraße, Friedrichshain . 317

318 . *Brandenburg Gate*, Pariser Platz, Mitte

Wilhelmstraße, Kreuzberg . 319

320 . *Haus der Kulturen der Welt*, John-Foster-Dulles-Allee, Tiergarten

Liquidrom, Möckernstraße, Kreuzberg . 321

322 . *Jewish Museum Berlin*, Lindenstraße, Kreuzberg

324 . Maybachufer, Neukölln

ICC, Masurenallee, Charlottenburg . 325

326 . Charlottenstraße, Mitte

328 . *Dome of the Reichstag*, Platz der Republik, Mitte

Alte Schönhauser Straße, Mitte . 329

330 . Alexanderplatz, Mitte

332 . Schiffbauerdamm, Mitte

Mehringdamm, Kreuzberg . 333

334 . *Brandenburg Gate*, Pariser Platz, Mitte

Oranienburger Straße, Mitte . 335

336 . Michaelbrücke, Mitte

338 . Hackescher Markt, Mitte

340 . *Berlin Central Station*, Mitte

Tempelhofer Park, Tempelhof . 341

342 . View towards Alexanderplatz, Mitte

Alexanderplatz, Mitte . 343

344 . Potsdamer Platz, Mitte

346 . Julie-Wolfthorn-Straße, Mitte

348 . Kurfürstendamm, Charlottenburg

Siegessäule, Großer Stern, Tiergarten . 349

350 . Tauentzienstraße, Charlottenburg

Spandauer Straße, Mitte . 351

352 . *Soviet War Memorial*, Tiergarten

Berlin Cathedral, Am Lustgarten, Mitte . 353

354 . Gendarmenmarkt, Mitte

Humboldt-Box, Schlossplatz, Mitte . 355

356 . *Molecule Man*, An den Treptowers, Treptow

358 . Wrangelstraße, Kreuzberg

Kurfürstendamm, Charlottenburg . 359

360 . Straße des 17. Juni, Tiergarten

Unter den Linden, Mitte . 361

362 . Straße des 17. Juni, Tiergarten

Ernst Reuter-Platz, Charlottenburg . 363

364 . *Reichstag*, Platz der Republik, Mitte

366 . Friedrichstraße, Mitte

Volkspark Friedrichshain, Danziger Straße, Prenzlauer Berg . 367

368 . Bergmannstraße, Kreuzberg

Karl-Liebknecht-Straße, Mitte . 369

370 . *Siegessäule*, Großer Stern, Tiergarten

TV-Tower, Alexanderplatz, Mitte . 371

372 . *Bellevue Palace*, Spreeweg, Tiergarten

Kastanienallee, Prenzlauer Berg . 373

374 . Potsdamer Platz, Mitte

Strausberger Platz, Friedrichshain . 375

376 . *Berlin Central Station*, Mitte

Alexanderplatz station, Mitte . 377

378 . Dianasee, Grunewald

Friedrichstraße, Mitte . 379

380 . View towards Oberbaum Bridge, Kreuzberg

View towards Oberbaum Bridge, Kreuzberg . 381

382 . Stralauer Allee, Friedrichshain

Auguststraße, Mitte . 383

384 . Columbiadamm, Tempelhof

Maybachufer, Neukölln . 385

386 . *Bellevue Palace*, Spreeweg, Tiergarten

Mauerpark, Prenzlauer Berg . 387

388 . *Reichstag*, Platz der Republik, Mitte

Oranienstraße, Kreuzberg . 389

390 . *Memorial to the Murdered Jews of Europe*, Ebertstraße, Mitte

Monument to the 1933 Book Burnings, Bebelplatz, Mitte . 391

hmmmm..... Lecker!

392 . Alexanderplatz, Mitte

Alexanderplatz, Mitte . 393

394 . Friedrichstraße, Mitte

Alte Schönhauser Straße, Mitte . 395

396 . Neue Schönhauser Straße, Mitte

East Side Gallery, Mühlenstraße, Friedrichshain . 397

398 . View towards *Bodemuseum* and Alexanderplatz, Mitte

Mauerpark, Prenzlauer Berg . 399

400 . *New Guard House*, Unter den Linden, Mitte

New Guard House, Unter den Linden, Mitte . 401

402 . *Kino International*, Karl-Marx Allee, Mitte

Zoo Palast, Hardenbergstraße, Charlottenburg . 403

404 . *Friedrichstadtpalast*, Friedrichstraße, Mitte

Berghain, Rüdersdorfer Straße, Friedrichshain . 405

406 . Christmas Market, Spandauer Straße, Mitte

Friedrichstraße, Mitte . 407

408 . *German Historical Museum*, Hinter dem Gießhaus, Mitte

25.9.1961

B 347

Fluchtversuch
und Festnahme,
Wilfried K.

410 . Schlesische Straße, Kreuzberg